CW00503849

John Higgs is the author of books including *The Future Starts Here*, *Watling Street*, *Stranger Than We Can Imagine* and *The KLF*. He lives in Brighton, England with his wife and their two children.

WILLIAM
BLAKE
NOW

Also By John Higgs

I Have America Surrounded
The KLF
Stranger Than We Can Imagine
Watling Street
The Future Starts Here

WILLIAM BLAKE NOW

Why He Matters More Than Ever

JOHN HIGGS

WEIDENFELD & NICOLSON

First published in Great Britain in 2019 by Weidenfeld & Nicolson
an imprint of The Orion Publishing Group Ltd
Carmelite House, 50 Victoria Embankment
London EC4Y 0DZ

An Hachette UK Company

1 3 5 7 9 10 8 6 4 2

A CIP catalogue record for this book is
available from the British Library.

ISBN (paperback) 9781474614337
ISBN (ebook) 9781474614344

Typeset by Input Data Services Ltd, Somerset

Printed and bound in Great Britain by Clays Ltd, Elcograf S.p.A.

MIX
Paper from
responsible sources
FSC® C104740

www.weidenfeldandnicolson.co.uk
www.orionbooks.co.uk

For Brian Barritt (1934–2011)

Contents

I

The Unveiling

Nick Duncan, the treasurer of The Blake Society, stands on a park bench in Bunhill Fields and looks at the sea of faces before him. 'There's a little more than the fifty or so people we were expecting,' he says, somewhat nervously. Those at the back of the vast crowd before him struggle to make out what he is saying. There is no microphone or public address system. No one had thought they would be necessary.

It is 12 August 2018 and the 191st anniversary of the death of the eighteenth-century poet, artist and printer William Blake. Blake was the author of such famous poems as 'The Tyger' and illuminated books such as *Jerusalem*, but during his lifetime he was mocked, ignored and pitied. He was written off as crazy, as much for his disturbing work as for his claims to see and converse with angels. After a lifetime of near poverty he was buried in a cheap, unmarked grave at the Bunhill Fields dissenters' graveyard in London, and the exact position of his remains was forgotten. Nearly two centuries later, the religious and political turmoil that fed his work has passed into irrelevancy. What could such a figure have to offer us here in the twenty-first century? Why would anyone care about William Blake now?

Yet here I am, drawn to this spot along with many hundreds of others, to witness the unveiling of Blake's new grave marker. Recent detective work has convincingly pinpointed the location of his remains and The Blake Society has raised money for a memorial – a flat piece of Portland stone, carved by the stonecutter Lida Cardozo Kindersley and set into the grass rather than standing tall like a gravestone.

The unveiling was not ticketed and there was no charge to attend. It was barely advertised. I heard about it from a tweet by The Blake Society, which gave details of the time and place, along with words: 'All are welcome!' Who could predict, in this modern age, how many people would assemble to witness the reveal of a new grave marker for a long-dead Georgian poet? Who would have expected the arrival of such huge crowds?

Looking around at the people who felt compelled to attend, I am struck by how hard to categorise they are. They seem to come from every sector of society. I see an elderly gent in a Barbour jacket and flat cap standing next to a teenage girl in a Metallica T-shirt. There is a lot of white hair, but there is pink hair also. The crowd seems to be roughly equally male and female, with a greater mix of ethnicities than I had expected. Small children run around the edges, while room is made for frail and elderly people who have made the effort to be here. Famous faces are scattered throughout the crowd. I realise with a shock that I am facing Philomena Cunk, also known as the comedian Diane Morgan, and I think I briefly see the actress Zoë Wanamaker.

I try to recall if I have ever been part of such a genuinely diverse crowd, because there is something unreal about seeing this collection of people together. It feels like we have been assembled for the purposes of an advert, and that the crowd has been deliberately engineered to exploit a half-remembered nostalgic ideal. We are in the middle of the Brexit years, a time of cultural and political division. The tribes don't mix like this anymore. And yet, here we all are. As The Blake Society declared – all are indeed welcome.

Blake's ability to reach across society like this is extremely unusual. His words to the hymn 'Jerusalem' have become the unofficial English national anthem, belted out with gusto by the flag-waving patriotic crowd at the finale of the Last Night of the Proms. The hymn's establishment credentials are strengthened through its adoption by the English cricket team and the Women's Institute, and its words were used by the post-war Labour prime minister Clement Attlee, one of the creators of the NHS and the welfare state, to describe the vision of Britain he was trying to build. Yet Blake is just as likely to be championed by anti-establishment figures such as Allen Ginsberg, Patti Smith or Billy Bragg, or played by colliery brass bands in solid working-class areas. What other artists can boast claims by both the establishment and the counterculture like this? Those who speak to the crowd ahead of the stone's unveiling include an academic, a theologian, the Rector of St James' Church, a punk poet, a comedian and a multi-millionaire heavy metal vocalist. The money to pay for the stone was raised by a benefit concert organised by the comedian Stewart Lee. It is strange that when a gravestone is needed for one of Britain's most notable poets of genius, the task of raising the money for it falls to a stand-up comedian.

There are marketing executives who would bottle Blake's secret, if only they could understand it. Businesses and artists invest a huge amount of effort in trying, and failing, to attract everybody. The wisdom of the age tells us that this can only be done by producing things that don't need imagination to be enjoyed. As the philosopher Chris Bateman wrote in 2010, talking about videogame design, 'In general terms, you can count on the formula "greater imagination required, smaller number of people attracted".' This formula explains the gulf between critical and commercial success in publishing, music, movies and many other fields, but it does not explain Blake. His appeal suggests that the opposite is true. His extraordinary, otherworldly work requires our imagination to appreciate it fully, often in quantities greater than most of us can provide. In theory, this should have condemned him to obscurity. Yet this strangely diverse crowd suggests that there is something about Blake that is important, and perhaps particularly so in times of division.

In January 2011, I visited the English Beat writer Brian Barritt in a south London hospital, just a few days before he died. He told me how the doctor had come to check on him early that morning and found him sat up in bed, singing and looking through a book of William Blake's artwork. The doctor, who had given Brian a terminal diagnosis the previous afternoon and told him that he only had days to live, viewed this behaviour as odd.

'He kept asking if I remembered him and what he told me yesterday,' Brian said. 'I explained that yes, I did. It's not the sort of conversation you forget. But he kept looking at me as if I didn't understand.' Brian shook his head. 'Honestly, John, where do you start with someone like that?'

For most people, this doctor would be an admirable figure. He was respected, experienced and worked long hours in an extremely emotionally challenging position for the good of the people of London. But to Brian, the fact that he couldn't understand that a man preparing to die would spend his last days reading Blake and singing meant that the doctor had gone wrong on a very profound level.

Towards the end of the Bunhill Fields gravestone unveiling, Brian comes to mind when I get the opportunity to place a candle at the side of the gravestone. I do this for him as much as for myself, for it was Brian who sparked my interest in Blake and insisted that I read him. Bending down with this small, flickering light, I am able to study the grave up close. 'Here lies WILLIAM BLAKE 1757–1827', it reads, 'Poet Artist Prophet'. That Blake's genius is considered to lie equally in his work as a visual artist and in his written words is, like his ability to be part of the establishment and the counterculture, an extremely rare quality that few others can claim.

Close to the stone, I notice a golden star carved between the words 'Poet' and 'Artist'. The star is so small that you are unlikely to notice it on photographs. It reminds me of an illustration from Blake's epic work *Milton: A Poem in 2 Books*. In that book, Blake is in the garden of his cottage in Felpham, Sussex, when the spirit of the poet John Milton falls from the sky in the form of a star and enters Blake by landing on his foot. For Blake, this was confirmation that he himself was part of a lineage of 'poetic genius' that stretches back over the ages.

It must have seemed an extraordinarily arrogant thing to claim at the time. Blake was then virtually unknown. His one solo art exhibition produced no sales and only one mention in the press, which described him as an 'unfortunate lunatic'. For Blake to describe himself as the natural successor of such an elevated poet must then have seemed delusional. Now, it is uncontroversial.

The engraving on the stone concludes with a quote from *Jerusalem*:

I give you the end of a golden string
Only wind it into a ball
It will lead you in at Heaven's gate
Built in Jerusalem's wall.

Those lines make explicit the promise Blake made to those who approach his work. He has found a way to a numinous place, and he wants us to accompany him. His work is a trail he has left and, if we follow it, it will lead us there.

For this gravestone unveiling, those words have been set to music by the Australian composer Chris Williams and are sung by the acapella choral ensemble Sansara. The members of the choir are scattered throughout the crowd, so that as you stand among this throng of people, voices come from all around you. From within the crowd, it feels like the voices of the singers have become the voice of the entire gathering, and as their harmonies rise and soar it is impossible not to raise your eyes and follow them upwards. High above us all are the branches of an enormous, ancient London plane tree, with its rich green sycamore-shaped leaves rustling gently in the summer air. Looking up at those branches with choral harmonies all around brings to mind William Blake as a boy around eight to ten years old, walking across what was then open countryside around Peckham Rye. There he looked up at a tree and saw a countless host of angels sat on the branches, glowing with a preternatural light, their 'bright angelic wings bespangling every bough like stars'.

With choral harmonies enveloping us, the idea that we can look up at this tree and see it through the eyes of Blake, if just for an instant, is hard to dismiss. The golden thread is at our feet, waiting for us. What is stopping us from picking it up? At this moment, I feel a sense that Blake is entirely present, and that his work is absolutely relevant to the twenty-first century. In this little book, I'll try to explain why I think that.

2

The Twentieth Century

After his pauper's burial in an unmarked grave, it must have seemed that William Blake would be forgotten. During his lifetime he was largely ignored by a culture that had no time for what he was trying to say. Awareness of him began to grow in the second half of the nineteenth century, thanks to the support of artists such as the Pre-Raphaelite Brotherhood and to Alexander's Gilchrist's 1863 book *Life of William Blake, 'Pictor Ignotus'* (the *pictor ignotus* in the title is Latin for 'unknown artist'.) His poems began to appear in Victorian anthologies, but his status remained obscure. A book about Blake published in 1904, Irene Langridge's *William Blake: A Study of his Life and Art Work*, tells us that 'three-quarters of a century have passed since the death of William Blake, and still his name and his work are but indifferently known.'

In the twentieth century, all this changed. A huge amount of academic research brought every detail of Blake's life and work into the light, and his influence escaped academia for an afterlife in popular culture. The most famous example of this is when Hubert Parry set Blake's words to music in the form of the hymn 'Jerusalem' and assigned the copyright to the National Union of Women's Suffrage Societies, but a deeper and stranger influence took hold in the middle of that century.

In 1948, the 22-year-old student Allen Ginsberg was lying on a bed in a rented apartment in Harlem, New York, experiencing something of a dark night of the soul. He had just received a letter from his sometimes-partner Neal Cassady, ending their relationship. As the legal guardian of his seriously ill mother, Naomi, he had signed a consent form that gave doctors permission to perform a lobotomy on her. His friends Jack Kerouac and William Burroughs were out of town and he was isolated. He would shortly be finishing college and was faced with the thorny issue of what to do with the rest of his life. As he recounted in a 1965 interview with *The Paris Review*, he had his trousers open and had just finished masturbating while he read William Blake's *Songs of Innocence and Experience*. (This may be too much information, but that's the Beat poets for you.)

He glanced down at the book, scanning the poem 'Ah! Sun-Flower'. It was so familiar to him that the poem barely registered. Then suddenly, somehow, the world changed, and he slipped into a state of bliss. He looked again at the poem, and he understood. As the poem's meaning arrived, he heard the voice of William Blake reading the words, communicating his intention to him directly. 'The voice was so completely tender and beautifully ancient. Like the voice of the Ancient of Days,' he later said. 'But the peculiar quality of the voice was something unforgettable because it was like God had a human voice, with all the infinite tenderness and anciency and mortal gravity of a living Creator speaking to his son.'

> Ah Sun-flower! weary of time,
> Who countest the steps of the Sun:
> Seeking after that sweet golden clime
> Where the travellers journey is done.

The sunflower, he realised, was him. It was he who was seeking that sweet golden clime. He looked out of the window, at the Harlem buildings outside and the sky above, and knew that his journey was done. That sweet golden clime was here. It was the world in which we live. It had been here all along, but he just needed to see it through the right eyes in the right state of mind. He just needed to experience this blissful state, which had arrived as if from nowhere.

Ginsberg looked at the cornices on the corners of the tenement building opposite and understood all that had happened to make them come into being. He recognised how many people had laboured to make them manifest, and he also realised how blind he had been not to see this before. 'Looking out at the window, through the window at the sky, suddenly it seemed that I saw into the depths of the universe, by looking simply into the ancient sky [. . .] This was the moment that I was born for. This initiation [. . .] There was a couple of girls living next door and I crawled out on the fire escape and tapped on their window and said, "I've seen God!" and they banged the window shut. Oh, what tales I could have told them if they'd let me in!'

This experience shaped the rest of Ginsberg's life. 'My first thought was this was what I was born for, and second thought, never forget—never forget, never renege, never deny. Never deny the voice.' He now had a purpose in life. He dedicated himself to poetry, in the hope of returning to the ecstatic state he felt reading Blake in that Harlem apartment.

In 1956 he published the poem 'Howl', the opening lines of which mixed his Blake vision with his experience of being placed in a mental institution after being expelled from Columbia University. *Howl and Other Poems* resulted in a prosecution for obscenity. The book's publisher Lawrence Ferlinghetti was arrested, along with a bookshop clerk who sold a copy of the book. Inspired by Blake's maxim that 'everything that lives is Holy!', Ginsberg had named some of the things that were holy, including the tongue, cock, hand and asshole. In a homophobic country just emerging from the McCarthy era, this and other similar sentiments were considered reason for prosecution. Ferlinghetti was acquitted, however, on the grounds that the poem had 'redeeming social importance'.

Ginsberg's search for ways to return to the bliss of his Blake vision led him, in 1960, to the Harvard psychologist Timothy Leary, who was then just starting to experiment with the little understood drugs LSD and psilocybin. Ginsberg took psilocybin at Leary's home and had an experience which, if not exactly the same as his Blake vision, was similar enough to seem like a major breakthrough. His reaction this time was not 'I've seen God', but, 'I am God!' This, at least, is what he told the telephone operator when he attempted to make calls to President Kennedy and Soviet leader Khrushchev while he was under the influence. More prophetically, the experience led to him telling Leary that what the world needed was a 'peace and love movement'.

Ginsberg became a key influence on Leary, as did the English writer Aldous Huxley, who was then a visiting lecturer at the Massachusetts Institute of Technology. Huxley had first experienced drug-induced states of altered consciousness in 1953, when he took mescaline. He detailed these experiences in his books *The Doors of Perception* (1954) and *Heaven and Hell* (1956). Through these books, Leary was inspired to contact Huxley.

As some of the earliest writing on what would soon be called 'psychedelic' drugs, Huxley's framing of the experience proved to be hugely influential, both on Timothy Leary and the wider counterculture that followed. Both the titles Huxley chose for his books were taken from Blake – Huxley had turned to Blake when he attempted to understand the experience of expanded awareness. A key idea that Huxley took from Blake was that the brain normally acts as a form of 'reducing valve' which limits how much of reality we perceive, and that certain drugs or mystical experiences could allow people to experience reality more fully. As Blake had written in *The Marriage of Heaven and Hell*, 'If the doors of perception were cleansed every thing would appear to man as it is, infinite./ For man has closed himself up, till he sees all things thro' narrow chinks of his cavern.'

William Blake soon became a constant presence in the memoirs of artists of this period. In one unforgivable example, the punk singer Patti Smith wrote about how her then partner, the photographer Robert Mapplethorpe, stole a print made from Blake's original plate. Mapplethorpe hid the print from *America: A Prophecy* down his trouser leg and made his escape from Brentano's, a historic American bookseller. He then felt so guilty about what he had done, and so afraid that he would be caught, that he went into a bathroom, retrieved the print from his trousers, ripped it into pieces and flushed William Blake down the toilet into the New York sewers below.

After Leary made the decision to promote LSD to the emerging generation, the 'peace and love movement' that Ginsberg had prophesised erupted on to the world stage. Given the influence of both Ginsberg and Huxley on Leary, and Leary's influence on people such as John Lennon, it is perhaps not surprising that Blake became absorbed into this counterculture, or that the aspects of William Blake that received the most attention were ones that reflected this culture.

When they looked to Blake, the 1960s counterculture focused on the side of him that was anti-authoritarian and individualistic. Statements such as 'Those who restrain desire, do so because theirs is weak enough to be restrained' were admired by a culture that saw sexual liberation as a political issue. Those in the drug culture approved of statements such as 'The road of excess leads to the palace of wisdom'. The Doors took their name from Blake's 'doors of perception' and quoted him directly in songs such as 'End of the Night'. Jimi Hendrix sang about his 'arrows of desire' on 'Voodoo Child' and Bob Dylan showed Blake influences in songs such as 'Visions of Johanna' and 'Every Grain of Sand'. Blake's cry of 'Rouze up, O Young Men of the New Age!', from the preface to *Milton,* echoed the counterculture's belief that they were entering a 'New Age', as described in songs such as 'Aquarius' from *Hair: The American Tribal Love-Rock Musical.*

The 1960s were a long time ago, however. We are in a very different world now. Calls for sexual liberation, anti-authoritarian individualism and a 'New Age' were important to people who lived through the stifling social conformity of the 1950s, but they can look a bit naïve and simplistic to those raised in the twenty-first century. The post-Millennial generation, or Generation Z as they are increasingly becoming known, take those advances for granted and typically have a far more nuanced and realistic understanding of them than people raised in the twentieth century did. Generation Z assume that sexual freedom is a given, for example, but they highlight the importance of consent in a way that the 1960s counterculture failed to do.

It might seem unlikely that the aspects of William Blake that the twentieth century focused on would be so important to those born or raised in the twenty-first. But Blake is nothing if not multi-faceted. The story of his post-death relevance is a long, shifting debate about the importance of different aspects of his personality. The radical, sexual, political, spiritual, individualist, republican, anarchic, alchemical, patriotic and creative sides to him have all been brought to the fore at various times, as our understanding of him increases.

So what will the twenty-first century make of William Blake?

3

London

On 28 November 2018, William Blake's 261st birthday, I paid a visit to the place where he was born. His family house had stood on the corner of Marshall Street and Broad Street (now Broadwick Street) in Soho, central London. If you go there now, you'll see a Patisserie Valerie standing on the spot.

I go in for tea and cake, hoping that I'll find some reference to Blake inside. Like the rest of the Patisserie Valerie chain, however, the interior is designed to reflect *Belle Époque* Paris, with posters by Henri de Toulouse-Lautrec and Jules Chéret adorning the walls. It's perfectly pleasant, but it ignores that this was the place where our national poet was born. It was here, at the age of four, that Blake saw the face of God through the upstairs window. In other cultures, I suspect, this location would be more celebrated.

The café is quiet and it is easy to find a table. Sitting down with my tea, I fall into watching the people hurrying past the window in the London streets outside. Most of them look harassed, and there is precious little joy evident on their faces. They bring to mind one of Blake's most famous poems, 'London':

> I wander thro' each charter'd street,
> Near where the charter'd Thames does flow.
> And mark in every face I meet
> Marks of weakness, marks of woe.
>
> In every cry of every Man,
> In every Infants cry of fear,
> In every voice: in every ban,
> The mind-forg'd manacles I hear.

The lines are still powerful, yet over the years the anger that fuelled the poem has become diluted. The poem has been assimilated into the established canon of English literature. Its period language gives it a sheen of respectability. How would it read, I wonder, if that safe, historical language was updated? It does not take much to convert the first stanza to contemporary English:

> I wander through each corporate street,
> Near where the corporate Thames does flow.
> And mark in every face I meet
> Marks of weakness, marks of woe.

Suddenly it has become a very different beast. It has become relevant again, and political. This is Blake in a nutshell: scrape away the patina of respectability and you find sparks and fury.

This is true even of the lines by Blake that have been absorbed into the very heart of the patriotic establishment, the words to the hymn 'Jerusalem'. When set to Sir Hubert Parry's stirring music, those words seem to rally support for our system and the English way of life. Yet when they are seen in their original context, in the preface to Blake's illustrated book *Milton*, they are suddenly a very different form of rallying cry. The paragraph that precedes 'And did those feet in ancient time' reads:

> Rouze up, O Young Men of the New Age! Set your foreheads against the ignorant Hirelings! For we have Hirelings in the Camp, the Court, & the University: who would if they could for ever depress Mental & prolong Corporeal War. Painters! on you I call. Sculptors! Architects! Suffer not the fash[i] onable Fools to depress your powers by the prices they pretend to give for contemptible works or the expensive advertizing boasts that they make of such works; believe Christ & his Apostles that there is a Class of Men whose whole delight is in Destroying.

This is a plea for the imagination needed to overthrow the existing, incompetent regime. Blake is gathering weapons of the mind, such as his 'arrows of desire', in order to replace the insipid, inadequate ruling classes with a visionary, elevated alternative. With this context, the words of the hymn take on an entirely new meaning. It is a cry of revolution.

I will not cease from Mental Fight,
Nor shall my Sword sleep in my hand,
Till we have built Jerusalem,
In England's green & pleasant Land.

There is a common belief among the more left-leaning, politically active Blakeans that the conservative, patriotic right doesn't really like Blake, as they claim they do. They just like the hymn 'Jerusalem', the argument goes, which they fail to understand. Yet the crowd at the unveiling of Blake's grave has made me question this. Those people, from all walks of life, were there because they had a connection to the man and his works that I could only see as genuine. They may not all have been attracted to the same aspects of him, but who is to say that some aspects are more valid than others? The idea that Blake is for everybody is not an idea that I am willing to discard just yet.

There is a strain in Blake, particularly in his early work, that could be called patriotism or nationalism, and which at times verges on jingoism. In 'A War Song to Englishmen', for example, he reacts to the realisation that he will be killed in battle fighting for his country by deciding that his life is a fair price to pay for England:

Why sinks my heart, why faultereth my tongue?
Had I three lives, I'd die in such a cause,
And rise, with ghosts, over the well-fought field.
Prepare, prepare.
[. . .]

Alfred shall smile, and make his harp rejoice;
The Norman William, and the learned Clerk,
And Lion Heart, and black brow'd Edward, with
His loyal queen shall rise, and welcome us!
Prepare, Prepare.

Perhaps Blake's most striking expression of nationalist pride is the satirical verse that begins 'When Klopstock England defied'. The Klopstock in question was Blake's near contemporary, the German poet Friedrich Gottlieb Klopstock, who is best known for his epic work *Der Messias* ('The Messiah'). Blake's verse was written in response to a minor slight Klopstock made about the English language. In response, 'English Blake', as he refers to himself, retaliates with an act of what can only be described as English voodoo shit magic. He starts by taking a crap under a poplar tree at Lambeth, but suddenly stands and spins round nine times, much to the disgust of the watching heavens. This act magically constricts Klopstock's bowels, causing him a great deal of pain, until Blake graciously undoes the spell. He then concludes:

If Blake could do this when he rose up from shite
What might he not do if he sat down to write

Yet as Blake matures, he quickly moves from a love of his own country to a love of all. He makes this evolution, from nationalism to the declaration that 'Everything that lives is Holy!', seem like a very natural progression.

In 'The Divine Image' from *Songs of Innocence*, he concludes:

> And all must love the human form,
> In heathen, Turk, or Jew;
> Where Mercy, Love, and Pity dwell
> There God is dwelling too.

In divided Brexit Britain, we usually think of nationalism and internationalism as opposites. Both sides tend to see their opponents in oversimplified or caricatured terms. Remainers portray the Leavers' love of country as inherently racist, and invariably connected to issues of immigration, cultural purity and about who decides who can be said to 'belong' here. Leavers, in contrast, portray that sense of belonging to a place as honest and natural, and a thing to be defended. For Remainers to deny that side of us is to deny human nature, they argue. These opposing positions can appear to be irreconcilable. Blake, however, had a great love of opposites. He saw them as a necessary step in moving forwards. As he wrote in *The Marriage of Heaven and Hell*, 'Without Contraries is no progression. Attraction and Repulsion, Reason and Energy, Love and Hate, are necessary to Human existence.' Or more enigmatically, 'Opposition is true Friendship.'

For Blake, the deep connection to the place around him was the soil in which a larger, spiritual love put down roots and grew to encircle the world. From this perspective, if you don't have love for your home and neighbours, then any proclamations of love for those further away is suspect. It is like someone who sees themselves as a good person because they express concern for an abstract group such as homeless people or refugees, yet who is a poor friend to the people they know and are in a position to help. And, conversely, if you condemn groups of strangers far away, then how true is your love for your home and neighbours really? Your antipathy to other people has to come from somewhere, and if it has not grown from your experiences with those that you do know, then where has it come from?

A sense of connection to your land, it can be argued, is necessary for, not opposed to, a deep respect for people of all cultures and creeds. This position goes past the framing of nationalism and internationalism, or leave and remain, as our primary duality. Instead, it divides the world into those who delight in what they love, and those who focus on what they hate.

This, it turns out, can be a far more useful guide to navigating our politics and culture.

4

Blake Now

Leaving the café, I turn right and walk to a set of
steps just behind it, in Marshall Street. These lead to
a sixteen-storey residential tower block called William
Blake House – a concrete modernist block, built in the
mid-1960s, which few would call lovely. It is, however,
the one thing around here that marks his birthplace, and
welcome for that reason. Here, on the small white tiles
alongside the steps, I find the following graffiti:

I DONATED PSYCHOACTIVE CHEMICALS AND PORNO-
GRAPHIC LITERATURE TO THE GRAVE OF WILLIAM
BLAKE AND ALL I GOT WAS MASSIVE GENTRIFICATION

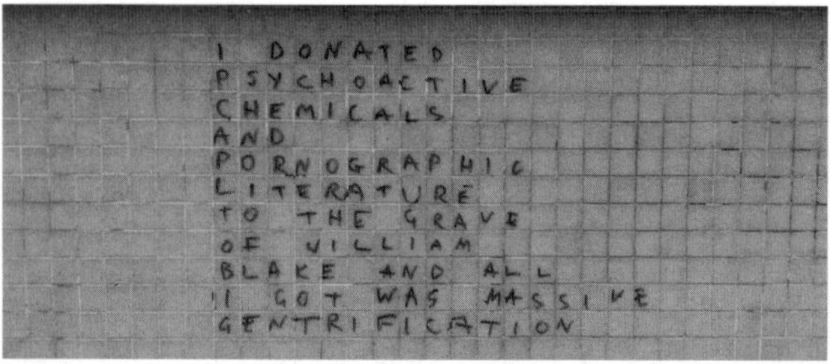

The establishment may not honour the spot where Blake was born, but memory of him enters the twenty-first century regardless. It seeps up from the streets, and oozes into the digital world, rather than being imposed from on high.

In 2018, the Blake scholar Professor Jason Whitaker monitored the number of mentions of the 'big six' Romantic poets on Twitter throughout the month of August. According to Whitaker, Coleridge came in last place, having received 1,559 mentions across the month. Then came Wordsworth (3,365), Shelley (5,692), Keats (6,823) and Byron (9,551). The winner was Blake, with 10,968 mentions. Blake, to be fair, had a number of advantages. He was not reliant on his fame as a poet, for his artwork was also being shared online. He had also written a number of short, shocking aphorisms, the Proverbs of Hell, which included lines such as 'Eternity is in love with the productions of time' and 'A fool sees not the same tree as a wise man sees.' These pithy, concise and dramatic slogans are ideally suited for sharing on social media. As Whitaker noted, the opinionated, brilliant Blake would have been great at Twitter.

Another appearance of Blake in twenty-first century culture, the likes of which someone such as Wordsworth cannot hope to compete with, can be found in the world of videogames. The May 2019 trailer for *A Plague Tale: Innocence*, for example, featured the actor Sean Bean reading Blake's poem 'Little Boy Lost'. The trailer appeared only a couple of months after the launch of the game

Devil May Cry 5. In this, the controls for one character included a button which, when pressed, caused them to recite William Blake, even in the midst of battle. This is not niche culture – the game claimed ecstatic reviews and sold over two million copies in the first two weeks on sale. At £50 per copy, it was a big deal.

Devil May Cry 5 opens with the words 'And it grew both day and night, Till it bore an apple bright', a quote from Blake's poem 'A Poison Tree'. Its relevance is soon revealed, as the story starts with a monstrous tree growing in the centre of a demon-infested London. At the heart of this poison tree sits a demon-king called Urizen, a character taken directly from Blake's own personal mythology.

The importance of Blake to *Devil May Cry 5* was apparent from the earliest trailers. It sent eager young gamers to Wikipedia and Google to learn who this Blake person was, and caused discussion on gaming forums about the exact nature of key characters in his work, such as Urizen, Los and Orc. For artists to enter the lives of new generations in this way, instead of being forced on them from authority figures in education, strikes me as healthy. When I played the game, however, a few doubts crept in. Not about the game itself, which plays beautifully, but about how helpful its use of Blake's iconography was.

The tone of the game is gleefully over the top. It starts with a sword that you can rev-up like a motorcycle and progresses until you are using a motorcycle as a sword.

The first playable character, an arrogant American with bleach-blond hair named Neo, is given truly terrible dialogue, such as 'Who brought the marshmallows? Because I'm bringing the fire!' If this had been a game developed in Britain by a company such as Rockstar North, you would interpret dialogue such as this as ironic or mocking. But although the game is set in Blake's London, it was developed by Capcom in Japan for Japanese and American audiences, so British levels of nuance or irony are not applicable here.

The core audience for the game are men in their thirties, especially those who played earlier *Devil May Cry* games when they were younger. The game's 18 certificate suggests that it is not officially aimed at the post-Millennial teenage Generation Z, but this fact is more readily apparent in its portrayal of women. There are women in the game, but you don't get to play as them. Instead, they are there to help you or to be rescued, and they are frequently naked or very underdressed. Gaming has its own norms, like any subculture, but the generation raised in the twenty-first century would not let this pass without comment.

After a few missions you get to play as a 'mysterious stranger' called V, a character who carries a volume of Blake's illuminated works with him everywhere he goes and quotes from it constantly. Ever since Rutger Hauer's character in the film *Blade Runner* enigmatically declared that 'Fiery the angels fell; deep thunder rolled around their shores; burning with the fires of Orc', which was a deliberate misquote of Blake's 'Fiery the angels rose' from *America: A Prophecy*, quoting Blake has been story shorthand for brooding villains who have depth, culture and sinister schemes.

V, unfortunately, looks like he would not be out of place in a Marilyn Manson or My Chemical Romance video from around 2003. He wears a long, sleeveless black coat which shows off his heavily tattooed arms, and he carries a cane. As one online reviewer put it, 'I'm not exactly taken with V's character design; he looks like that rich literature student sitting at the back of the class who discovered his Tory Grandfather's cane in the attic and blew his trust fund on early 2000's tribal tattoos. You know the one [. . .] He's good looking in that crooked nose, unkempt hair and starved for food Brexit British way.' Before I read this review, I hadn't realised that 'Brexit' had already become international shorthand for starving.

In the middle of a game, as you slaughter demons left, right and centre, these ludicrous characters make total sense. You are too caught up in the hyper-realised world to question them. But when the game is over, you realise that Blake was being used as nothing more than window dressing for an emo power fantasy. What is important about him, the aspect of his work that the twenty-first century needs, is conspicuous by its absence.

The use of Blake in *Devil May Cry 5* is similar to his use by Thomas Harris in his novel *Red Dragon*.

Introducing the world to the character of Hannibal Lecter, the novel has been twice adapted for the screen. It features a disturbed serial killer who is obsessed by Blake's watercolour painting 'The Great Red Dragon and the Woman Clothed in Sun', and who has his back tattooed so that he resembles the red dragon. At one point in the story, in a scene that might make even Robert Mapplethorpe wince, the serial killer goes to the Brooklyn Museum to see the original watercolour, then stuffs it in his mouth and eats it.

In *Red Dragon*, Blake is used as shorthand for something mad and frightening. When the detective realises the importance of Blake to the case and investigates further, his work is presented as exactly the sort of thing deranged serial killers would be into. *Devil May Cry* uses it in a similar way, as little more than a form of Goth window dressing.

Could this be the fate of Blake in the twenty-first century; a source of dark horror to be mined for heavy metal lyrics, videogames and horror movies? It might not be the aspect of Blake that polite society dwells upon, but there is certainly a vein of highly-strung demonic horror in his work. You can dismiss *Devil May Cry*'s portrayal of Urizen as much as you like, but tonally the game is not far from Blake's *The First Book of Urizen*, which begins with the words 'Lo, a shadow of horror is risen/ In Eternity!' Consider, for example, how Blake describes the formation of Urizen's body:

In a horrible, dreamful slumber;
Like the linked infernal chain,
A vast Spine writh'd in torment
Upon the winds, shooting pain'd
Ribs, like a bending cavern;
And bones of solidness froze
Over all his nerves of joy.
And a first Age passed over,
And a state of dismal woe.

Our culture tends to look down on these things, but Blake is absolutely a source of melodramatic Gothic horror, which is an aspect of his work that can be enjoyed and celebrated. The problem is that there is much more to Blake than this surface horror. His depths are missing from media such as *Red Dragon* and *Devil May Cry*, but do they have to be missing from our culture as a whole?

5

Understanding Blake

The reason why spooky, shallow versions of Blake are so common in our culture is that very few people understand his depths. His mythology is not currently a shared cultural touchstone that filmmakers, authors and game designers can expect their audience to know. His work is perceived as being too complicated and, in places, incomprehensible. A frequently repeated truism, used even by Blake scholars, is that 'nobody really understands Blake'.

The first admission of an inability to understand Blake was probably that of his wife, Catherine. She is recorded as saying that she did not always understand her husband's writings, 'though she was sure that they had a meaning, and a fine one'. Often, this admission comes with a belief that it is other people who get him wrong. As the post-punk musician Jah Wobble said, 'I don't think anybody really understands Blake [. . .] He's been hijacked by retired colonels in Surrey who think he represents their Albion, and he absolutely doesn't.'

You will hear it said that the key to Blake was that he was either a political radical, or a traditionalist; a libertarian, or a socialist; a pious Christian, or a free-love heretic; a nationalist patriot, or an internationalist; a madman, or the only sane person in the eighteenth century. His biographer Peter Ackroyd writes that 'it can truly be said that he is the last great religious poet in England', but others see Blake as far ahead of his time, not behind it. In a speech to mark the opening of a Blake exhibition at The Whitworth Art Gallery in 2008, the musician Julian Cope, describing the cultural changes of post-war Western civilisation as a great storm pounding across the landscape, said that, 'William Blake was like a single cloud running ten miles ahead, throwing down rain and hail before the storm's main body had even broken the horizon.' The difficulty of reconciling all these contradictory perspectives on his work creates the strange situation where many people will tell you that they love Blake, yet they make no effort to read him.

Of all the speakers at the gravestone unveiling, the one that I was most surprised to see was the heavy metal vocalist Bruce Dickinson. By coincidence, I had seen Dickinson and his band Iron Maiden on stage at London's O2 Arena the previous night, delivering a stadium-sized performance to tens of thousands of ecstatic metal fans. It was quite a show. It began with a life-sized Spitfire plane hovering above the stage and the spectacle, flames and explosions only increased from there on in. Dickinson had a sword fight with a giant undead soldier, wore two flamethrowers, one on each arm, and ended the concert by blowing up the stage with a Wile E. Coyote-style detonator. On stage, he was about eight foot tall. He was the last person I expected to see at Blake's grave the following day, and I couldn't understand why he was now only 5'6".

Dickinson told the crowd at Bunhill Fields about his lifelong love of Blake, and how much the poet had influenced his work. He explained that the reason he wrote new music for the poem 'Jerusalem' was because he disliked how jingoistic the existing music was, and how the hymn misunderstood what Blake's words were about. Later, the original version of the song was performed by the side of the grave by the classical vocal harmony group Blake, which consisted of three well-scrubbed ex-public schoolboys in sharp suits. I distinctly saw Dickinson roll his eyes at this point.

In his autobiography, Dickinson talks about how he fell 'under the spell of the difficult, curmudgeonly but otherworldly Blake'. But unusually, he portrays the 'difficult' nature of Blake's work as an interesting challenge, and something that can be grasped and understood. 'I was struck by his two characters Los and Urizen,' he wrote. 'Los (or Sol backwards) was creative and doomed forever to have his head buried in a bucket of fire, symbolising the torture of the endlessly creative soul [. . .] I had some inkling of what it felt like to love the creativity but be held back by the grim realities of the commercial and the fear of change. I could relate to Blake.' You might say it is not surprising that a man who wears a flamethrower on each arm would identify with a character with his head on fire, but Dickinson's album *The Chemical Wedding* displays a deep, if always playful, knowledge of the rest of Blake's mythology. Dickinson sees engaging with the mysteries of Blake as exciting, and nothing to be scared of.

This 'can do' attitude to approaching Blake reminds us that to understand him is not a binary, yes/no position. It is not like understanding long division or the offside rule, which is something you either can or can't do. Instead, it is more like understanding a musical instrument. There are some basics that you need to grasp at the beginning, but from there you set out on a long journey of discovery. Masters of an instrument insist that they are still learning and discovering new things even at the very end of their lives.

Understanding Blake is not knowledge you possess, but an activity that you undertake. You do not need permission, and you can start at any age. Ironically, the difficult nature of his work has helped make the Blake world feel relatively inclusive and welcoming. Ignorance is assumed, rather than something to be ashamed of.

There are many fantastical mythologies which become so sufficiently well known that they turn into cultural touchstones. We expect most people to know who Merlin, Gandalf, Iron Man, Dumbledore or Yoda are. Blake's intricate personal mythology is slightly different, in that it is not as plot based as most mythologies. Few would say that Blake's main strength was that he tells a good yarn. Yet they are absolutely characters who we can understand and become familiar with, if we choose to do so. His characters are both individual spirits and a part of ourselves at the same time. Because of this, they have one advantage that more familiar mythological characters may lack. Because they are part of us, when we do grasp them, we understand them intimately.

In the twentieth century, we favoured simple stories which frequently fitted the 'Hero's Journey' structure, as described by the American academic Joseph Campbell. These were stories about a lone, brave individual overcoming terrible odds to emerge with a great prize, alongside an almost child-like cast of simplified good guys and bad guys. But here in the twenty-first century, our tastes have changed. Now we want to explore whole worlds. We lose ourselves for years in the complex politics of the land of Westeros, and we follow the huge, interconnected casts of the Marvel Cinematic Universe. We are drawn to stories that take decades to tell. Depth isn't a barrier anymore. Depth is a draw.

The idea that Blake is too strange and too incomprehensible to get to grips with was common in the twentieth century. I don't think that's the case anymore. True, it would take a larger book than this one to do justice to the richness of his mythology, but such a book would repay your efforts a thousand times over. There is an extraordinary world to be found in the work of William Blake, and there is nothing stopping you from entering it.

6

On Being Remembered

To artists, Blake can be something of a double-edged sword. Like Van Gogh, he is a universally recognised genius who was entirely dismissed in his own time. This makes him a powerful archetype. It can give artists encouragement to keep working during periods when they receive little encouragement. It can, however, be used as an excuse. The danger is that artists might not hone their work to the point where it communicates to others, in the belief that their singular genius will be recognised after they die. It is true that the act of creating something is valid and rewarding regardless of the audience awaiting it, but it is also true that work needs to affect others if it is to be considered truly great.

In 2017, I went to the Tate Liverpool to see a joint exhibition of works by Tracey Emin and William Blake. When I first heard about the show, I wondered if somebody at the Tate had a grudge against Emin. Few current artists could hold their own against Blake, but Emin in particular did not seem like she would come out of the comparison well.

I assumed that the juxtaposition was to contrast two of the most different artists that they could find. Blake is a dead, male artist, while Emin is a living, female artist. Emin has been embraced by the art establishment and become incredibly wealthy, while Blake was ignored and practically penniless. Emin is a monarchist and a Conservative, while Blake was a republican and a revolutionary. Blake spent his life railing against hypocrisy and injustice, while Emin once complained about having to pay tax at the 50 per cent rate. Blake was tried for sedition and was in danger of being hanged, while Emin's reputation for danger is largely based on an incident in 1997 when she appeared on a TV programme drunk. Blake's work focuses on a bewilderingly elaborate universal mythology of his own devising, while Emin focuses on herself to an almost tabloid level, most famously in work such as 'Everyone I Have Ever Slept With 1963–1995', which consisted of a tent with the names of all the people she had shared a bed with sewn inside. Tracey Emin and William Blake, clearly, are very different artists.

According to discussions surrounding their joint exhibition, however, the show existed to reveal their similarities. 'Join us for *Tracey Emin and William Blake In Focus* and discover surprising links between the two artists', began the Tate's introduction; 'this free exhibition compares important works from the Tate collection, demonstrating a shared concern with birth, death and spirituality in both artists' work'. This is fair enough, although it would be a challenge to find an artist who didn't also make reference in their work to birth, death or spirituality.

Yet comparisons between Blake and Emin have a long history and, despite what I initially assumed, they do not appear to be sarcastic. As Emin's biographer Neal Brown noted in 2006, 'To say that Emin is like Blake, as has often been done, is not to claim that she is his equal. But it is true that she, like him, is a romantic who, although admired by many, has also disturbed people to the point of fear [. . .] Both artists, in their search for poeticised truth, manifest a strong disregard of opinion, so putting them in conflict with the sexual sensibilities and spiritual beliefs of others.'

I entered the exhibition hoping that the reasons for these comparisons would reveal themselves. The main room was dominated by Emin's most famous work, 'My Bed', which was first exhibited by the Tate gallery in 1999 when Emin was nominated for the Turner Prize. With the bed being so prominently displayed in the centre of the room, you could not help but approach it first when you entered.

I glanced over the unkempt, dirty bed surrounded by condoms, overflowing ashtrays and other detritus and thought, 'Well, we've all been there.' Then I wandered off to look around the rest of the exhibition. There I found the small framed Blake prints and watercolours around the walls, like little windows into another world. If my visit to the exhibition was anything to go by, my behaviour was fairly typical. Visitors would walk in, look at the bed for a few seconds, then turn away and lose themselves in the Blakes for the rest of their visit.

There are artists who become successful and celebrated through being in sync with their times, yet who hold little interest to generations that follow. Blake's friend the sculptor John Flaxman, for example, was one of the most famous and influential artists of his day. He is almost entirely forgotten now, while Blake has gone from obscurity to global renown. In a similar way, the work that made Emin's name captured the essence of 1990s Britain perfectly. You could imagine 'My Bed' being created as an album cover for a Britpop band such as Pulp. Whether it will remain important to generations to come is hard to say.

There are already signs that Emin's work is of little importance to those who are not financially invested in it. When her tent and other works were destroyed in a fire at an east London warehouse in 2004, Emin was angry and upset about the lack of sympathy shown by the wider public and by newspapers such as the *Daily Mail*. People generally seemed to think that the fact her most famous artwork had been destroyed was quite funny. This was harsh, but it is true that hearing about the loss of her tent does not usually generate the same gut-level horror as hearing about Robert Mapplethorpe ripping up a Blake and flushing it down the toilet.

It is, however, unfair to unflatteringly compare work that is solely about the time it was made to work that remains powerful over centuries. We tend to value and celebrate direct, clear lineages and influences between the pantheon of the great artists going back centuries, because this is what art histories focus on. Yet the influences of an artist who is only briefly in vogue can have a more significant influence on their culture, even if those influences are less distinct and harder to define.

When an artist such as John Flaxman or members of the 1990s YBA movement achieve great success in their time, they have a small impact on hundreds of thousands of people rather than a large impact on art history. These hundreds of thousands of slight influences are not as easy to quantify as a small number of clear, distinct influences, but their cumulative impact on culture as a whole can be considerably greater. That they disappear after flaring up into a dazzling but brief supernova is nothing to be ashamed of – it is the countless small influences on countless different people that matters.

A key factor here is the artist's ego. By this I'm not referring to the artist's vanity, but instead to the bundle of opinions, ideas, experiences and perspectives that make up who they are. These are the things that the artist believes are so important that they need to be inflicted on the wider world. Financial reality, which requires the artist to become a distinct 'brand' in the eyes of the wider audience, pushes them to strengthen and protect that delicate ego of bundled thoughts.

Yet the point of producing and sharing work is the opposite of this. When your opinions, ideas, experiences and perspectives get dissolved into the wider culture, there is no longer the need to cling on to them. That bundle of thoughts gets slowly dissolved into the great ocean of wider culture, and the need for the artist's ego to protect them falls away. From this perspective, the real goal of an artist is to dissipate into nothing and be forgotten. As Blake wrote in *Milton*, 'I come to Self Annihilation / Such are the Laws of Eternity, that each shall mutually/ Annihilate himself for others good'.

There are many reasons why certain artists are re-membered and become fixed in the pantheon instead of dissolving away. The primary reason is a body of work that is both extensive and consistently brilliant. This is why Shakespeare and Dickens are known by all, while even the best of their contemporaries are only known to specialists. Class, gender and ethnicity can also be considered factors, due to the systematic prejudices of the art establishment. Sometimes charisma can be what makes the difference. As good as it was, the work of people such as Oscar Wilde, Jimi Hendrix or Kurt Cobain might already have become a footnote in our artistic history had it not been for their blazing charm and tragic ends. Then there are people who puzzle and intrigue us, who we can't quite understand. These people are sometimes too fascinating to be forgotten.

Blake manages to fit into all these categories, giving him many paths into the pantheon of the greats. Yet in one important way he has more in common with the artists who focus on their own time and whose influence is diluted and widespread. His output was vast, involved and complicated, but there is a core idea that lies at the heart of his work. It is an idea that has spread through our culture in the same diverse, widespread and untraceable way that forgotten artists influence the world. It is the reason why Blake keeps bubbling back into our culture through unpoliced mediums such as graffiti or video-games, rather than through establishment endorsement.

The idea is this: the human imagination is divine.

7

Once Only Imagin'd

Blake was born in the Age of Enlightenment, which rejected the medieval idea that our most important value was faith. Instead, reason was declared to be primary. Only reason could trump faith.

For Blake, this wasn't going far enough. Reason was important, but it was only a small, bounded part of what the mind was capable of. Blake recognised that it was imagination, not reason, that was fundamental, because reason was only a product of the imagination. As he describes the situation, 'What is now proved was once only imagin'd.' We use reason to understand the world, but it only shows us a tiny part of what is out there. When we become stuck, we have to go outside of established reasoning in order to find answers. Here Blake's position was similar to that of Albert Einstein, who said that 'Imagination is more important than knowledge. For knowledge is limited, whereas imagination embraces the entire world, stimulating progress, giving birth to evolution.'

It's worth stressing, however, that Blake's understanding of imagination is different to how the word is typically understood today. If you ask someone in the twenty-first century what the word 'imagination' means, they will probably say that it is just making stuff up. This is not how the word used to be understood.

According to the Romantic poet Samuel Taylor Coleridge, there was an important difference between fantasy and imagination. Fantasy was indeed 'just making stuff up', he thought. It was essentially a form of mental collage – taking existing ideas and putting them together, in a way that was unrelated to the real world of time and space. You could take the idea of a horse and the idea of a horn, stick them together as a form of collage, and you had the fantasy of a unicorn in a world where no physical unicorns existed.

This was fine, as far as it goes. Fantasy could be entertaining in its own right. But it is unconnected to reality. It doesn't change things. It doesn't matter.

Imagination was something different. Imagination was the arrival, from the depths of consciousness, of something genuinely new. True, it might contain things that already exist, but they had now become part of something larger, and unprecedented. Coleridge invented the word 'esemplastic' to describe this process, in which separate elements are combined to create something entirely original. Fantasy was just the same old stuff rearranged with a healthy disregard for the real world. Imagination, in contrast, was engaging with existing stuff to produce something never seen before. This, being brand new, had the power to change the

JOHN HIGGS

world in a way that fantasy did not. Something new
now existed, and the world had to adapt around it.

Imagination had a vivid quality that fantasy lacked.
In fantasy, a thought was just a thought. In deep imagination, a thought was something that you encountered.
It was participatory. It was a living, vital process that
you were part of. You were not separate from what you
imagined, and imagination was not separate from the
world, because the world and imagination could not be
understood without each other.

Recall that Blake used the metaphor of the 'doors of
perception' being cleansed, rather than the more logical
metaphor of the 'windows of perception'. A window,
after all, was something that you could see through,
and which could become dirtied and opaque. At first,
it seems to be the ideal choice here, because there were
no such things as glass doors in Blake's day. Yet Blake
chose a door because while we look through windows,
we pass through doors, in both directions.

For Blake, everything came from the imagination.
As he wrote in *Jerusalem*, '. . . in your own Bosom you
bear your Heaven/ And Earth, & all you behold, tho' it
appears Without it is Within/ In your imagination'. It
is from the infinite realm of imagination that our finite,
limited world emerges. Being the source of everything,
it was also the source of the divine. Heaven and Hell,
grace and torment, Jesus and Satan – they were all prod-
ucts of the mind. This is very different to saying that
they don't exist.

Thanks to the hymn 'Jerusalem', Blake is usually portrayed as a committed Christian and a believer in God, but the name he gives the god of the established Church – Nobodaddy – suggests that things aren't quite so clear cut as this. As he wrote in 'The Everlasting Gospel':

> The Vision of Christ that thou dost see
> Is my visions Greatest Enemy [. . .]
> Both read the Bible day & night
> But thou readst black where I read white

Blake understood that the gods come from us, and not vice versa. As he wrote in *The Marriage of Heaven and Hell*, 'Thus men forgot that All deities reside in the human breast.' When the diarist Henry Crabb Robinson asked Blake about the divinity of Jesus Christ in 1825, he replied 'He is the only God', but then added, much to Crabb Robinson's confusion, 'And so am I and so are you.' Crabb Robinson didn't know what to make of this. He did not understand that the Jesus whom Blake worshipped was 'Jesus, the imagination', or that he believed that it was not just the historical figure of Jesus who could experience the consciousness of Christ. Being a product of the mind, this Christ consciousness was theoretically available to all, as Ginsberg's experience in his New York tenement in 1948 shows.

During the religious turmoil of the 1790s, a self-proclaimed prophet named Richard Brothers promised to lead the faithful back to the city of Jerusalem. But

47

Blake knew that Jerusalem, in the religious sense, was not a place you had to journey to. Wherever we are can become the holy city, if we see it in the correct state of mind. Blake talks about building Jerusalem on Albion's rocky shore not because there is something special about Britain, but because that was where he was. The idea applies equally to all other parts of the world.

In standard theology, Hell is a place that exists somewhere, external to us. For Blake, it is something that we construct inside ourselves when we close ourselves off from other people. In *Milton*, he describes Satan building Hell inside himself as he turns opaque and hides his inner light from those around him. Even in the secular twenty-first century, this is an idea that still resonates. We may not believe that Hell is a real place that exists somewhere, but we have probably all met someone who is living in hell.

Just as Blake offered us a way past the seemingly irreconcilable divide of nationalism and internationalism, here he offers us a way past the divide between those who are atheists and those who believe in a spiritual dimension to life. It is perhaps fitting that the president of The Blake Society is the author Philip Pullman, a man whose campaigning for atheist causes might initially make him seem a strange choice to represent such a spiritual artist. The idea that divinity exists and is a product of the human imagination can be embraced by believers and agnostics alike. It does not require the wholesale junking of our rich theological history, and neither does it offer support for persecutions undertaken with religious justification.

Some might argue that this belittles divinity. It is more accurate, I think, to say that it raises up our understanding of the imagination.

8

On Primrose Hill

At the top of Primrose Hill, just to the north of Regents Park in London, is a plaque that commemorates the eighteenth-century Welsh antiquarian and cofounder of modern Druidry, Iolo Morganwg. '*Yma y cyfaifu Gorsedd Beirdd Ynys Prydain gyntaf*', states the plaque in Welsh, with the English translation: 'This is the site of the first meeting of the Gorsedd of the Bards of the Isle of Britain.' The use of Welsh in this affluent London suburb might seem out of place, but the first people who lived in this landscape would have spoken the proto-Welsh language Common Brittonic. It was on this site, at sunrise on the summer solstice in 1792, that the Bardic tradition of these islands was reborn.

When the plaque was unveiled in 2009, members of the well-to-do Friends of Regents Park and Primrose Hill were far from happy. An editorial in their magazine was titled 'Iolo – Who He?' It complained that: 'This chap was bankrupt and a forger. A bloody criminal. This plaque has just appeared out of nowhere. It is a diabolical cheek.' Primrose Hill is an exclusive, upmarket area, and Morganwg struck certain residents as being the 'wrong sort'. Fortunately, the Royal Parks, who had given permission to install the plaque, had a deeper understanding of British History. They wisely ignored the complaints.

There have been attempts made to place William Blake at this first midsummer Druid ceremony, but his presence there seems unlikely. It is true that Blake lived at 28 Poland Street between 1785 and 1790, which was only two doors away from the pub where Lodge Number 1 of the Ancient Order of Druids held their meetings. But Blake was not one for joining societies. He did mention Druids in his work, but he was not always complimentary. Druidry smacked too much of priesthood for his liking. Nevertheless, he is present at Primrose Hill now. In 2012, his words were carved around the edge of the circular, paved summit. They read: 'I have conversed with the Spiritual Sun – I saw him on Primrose Hill.' This Blake connection is why Allen Ginsberg climbed Primrose Hill during his visit to Britain in 1967, where he was filmed discussing Blake while wearing a red silken shirt featuring symbols hand-painted by Paul McCartney. Ginsberg then headed to Wales, following the spirit of Morganwg, where he wrote the poem 'Wales – A Visitation'.

I visit Primrose Hill on a spring day in 2019. Young people are scattered around the grass and countless dog walkers patrol the paths. A group of friends toss around a frisbee while playing children ignore public schoolboys loudly broadcasting some particularly misogynistic rap music. It is April, and only half the trees are in leaf, yet the day is so unnaturally hot that it feels like the height of summer. Our weather has become extreme, and the physical sun, if not the spiritual one, is making itself known.

Blake refers to the notion of a different, more important sun in verse from a letter to his patron Thomas Butts in November 1802.

> My hands are labour'd day and night
> And Ease comes never in my sight
> My Wife has no indulgence given
> Except what comes to her from Heaven
> We eat little, we drink less
> This Earth breeds not our happiness
> Another Sun feeds our lifes streams

Or, as he describes it in *Jerusalem: The Emanation of The Giant Albion,*

> Then the Divine Vision like a silent Sun appeard above
> Albions dark rocks: setting behind the Gardens of
>   Kensington

This other sun was the blazing light of the imagination. Those who could not see it pitied Blake, because to them he appeared to be nothing more than a penniless, crazy artist. If they had caught just a glimpse of this different sun, they would have understood why Blake saw material wealth and success as secondary.

I look down the hill towards the London skyline. It is perhaps twenty years since I last came up here, and the skyline has noticeably changed. Many of the additions are not the rectangular, squat tower blocks of before, but buildings that now curve and bulge in strange proportions. One thing that has not changed, however, is the swarm of cranes which sprout from the skyline. I used to think that these spoiled the view, but now I understand that the view wouldn't exist without them. London is a living thing, like a forest. It is in a state of constant change, a process and not an object. Many people over the centuries have declared the end of London, but the city always ignores them and continues as before. If the cranes were to vanish from this view, only then would I believe that the end of London is at hand.

I think back to my earlier attempts to update the poem 'London'. The first verse had been relatively easy, and any changes to the second beyond modern spelling or grammar seemed unnecessary.

> I wander through each corporate street,
> Near where the corporate Thames does flow.
> And mark in every face I meet
> Marks of weakness, marks of woe.
>
> In every cry of every Man,
> In every Infants cry of fear,
> In every voice, in every ban,
> The mind-forged manacles I hear.

'The mind-forged manacles' is too good a phrase to change, but it could be updated to become more relevant to the emerging twenty-first century culture. The phrase tells us that what is holding us back and constraining others is our thoughts and our established ways of thinking. Generation Z, those born or raised in the twenty-first century, understand this. In their parlance, realising this is to become 'woke'.

The third verse is the verse that has perhaps aged the most:

> How the Chimney-sweepers cry
> Every blackning Church appalls,
> And the hapless Soldiers sigh
> Runs in blood down Palace walls

Here 'appalls' is used in an eighteenth-century way to mean 'to shame', while the Church, soldiers and palace are institutions of control which don't quite have the same meaning. The media, police and Westminster would perhaps be their modern equivalents. The chimney sweepers mentioned in the first line is a reference to the cruelty of child labour, and these days we are careful to ensure that any child labour that supports our lifestyles takes place in foreign countries. Any ham-fisted attempt I make to update this verse quickly collapses into polemic, and the power and grace of Blake's lines are lost. Instead, I turn to the fourth verse. This is the one that has traditionally given scholars the most trouble.

> But most thro' midnight streets I hear
> How the youthful Harlots curse
> Blasts the new-born Infants tear
> And blights with plagues the Marriage hearse

The main difficulty with this verse is that most people do not want to think about what it is clearly referring to. 'Youthful Harlots' means child prostitutes; Blake's 'London' depicts a place where men catch venereal diseases from child prostitutes and pass them on to their wives. This is an aspect of Regency England that most of its writers, and indeed readers, would prefer to ignore. Blake, in contrast, could not ignore it. He lived in Lambeth just around the corner from the old Hercules Inn. It was converted in 1758 into the Female Orphan Asylum in order to save girls aged between nine and twelve from prostitution. This was the city he knew, and it made him angry.

In the 4 December 1791 edition of the *Observer*, we read that: 'A west-country gentleman, not much acquainted with the ways of London, expressed great surprise, a few nights ago, at the *flocks* of *chicken prostitutes* which he observed before Somerset House, and which he actually mistook for the pupils of some large boarding-school. One of the young *misses*, however, soon convinced him of his error, by granting a favour, which will probably retard his journey home for some time.' Here the existence of child prostitution is acknowledged, but the incident is played for laughs. There is no anger, or empathy, or demands for change. This is what makes Blake different to his contemporaries. When he saw how the London establishment calmly accepted child chimney sweeps and child prostitutes, he condemned the Church and the ruling elite for accepting it. He did not simply ignore the problem, as most others did.

My journey to Primrose Hill was complicated by a two-week period of ongoing demonstrations by the Extinction Rebellion group. They had taken over Parliament Square, Waterloo Bridge, Marble Arch and Oxford Circus, stopping traffic and holding non-violent protests, and they had glued themselves to trains and the entrance to the London Stock Exchange. Over a thousand people were arrested, most willingly, in a police response that involved the deployment of 10,000 officers. I encountered them at Oxford Circus, where they had parked a pink sailboat in the crossroads of Oxford Street and Regent Street. The atmosphere at the protest was incredibly welcoming and positive, a far cry from the sense of potential violence that can be found on other demonstrations. The average age of those at the protest was also far younger than usual.

That these demonstrations disrupted travel for countless Londoners resulted in a lot of criticism from various politicians and media commentators. This was ironic, as the failure of those same politicians and media commentators to engage with the climate problem was what prompted the protests. I think again of the words of Blake: 'Without Contraries is no progression.' Staying neutral and placid is not how we advance. Stopping London traffic for a week and causing extensive disruption will generate a huge backlash, but it will advance the issue in a way that doing nothing will not. Within a couple of weeks of the protest, the House of Commons declared there was a climate emergency, as did the Welsh and Scottish parliaments. This was something that decades of polite, democratic campaigning had failed to achieve. As the Banksy graffiti that appeared at Marble Arch during the protest stated, 'From this moment despair ends and tactics begin.'

I look again at the plaque to Iolo Morganwg atop Primrose Hill, which so angered the contented and affluent local residents, and read his most famous words, which are etched underneath his portrait: '*Y gwir yn erbyn y byd*' – 'The truth against the world.'

Over two hundred years later, those words seem entirely apt for the protests currently blocking the city. For all that many people criticise the protestors themselves, there are few who can criticise their cause. Like the suffragettes or the American Civil Rights Movement, they are unarguably on the right side of history. They have the science and the research to back their case, and the unseasonal extreme heat of the day emphasises the urgency. Like Blake condemning child labour and child prostitution, they are saying what needs to be said at a time when the bulk of society prefer to close their eyes and not think about the wrongs going on around them.

When academics attempt to label the prevailing

attitudes of the world as it is now, they increasingly use the word 'metamodern'. Metamodernism is, they tell us, what has replaced postmodernism. It refers to the flight to extremes, and in particular to seemingly contradictory extremes, in order to achieve things that a reasoned, centrist, calm negotiation cannot. I mentioned earlier how Blake is seen as both a political radical and a traditionalist, a libertarian and a socialist, a pious Christian and a free-love heretic. His willingness to explore what is useful in seemingly opposite extremes makes him almost a textbook definition of metamodernism, as does his statement that 'Without Contraries is no progression.' In this way he is entirely in tune with contemporary times. It has taken us a while, but we are finally catching up with him.

Metamodern culture is chaotic and worrying, with a tendency to veer towards tribalism and animosity. The Trump presidency and Brexit are obvious examples. For those of us raised in the postmodern twentieth century, it can be deeply disturbing. But to the post-Millennial generation, this is all they have known. To them, this is just how the world works. That Generation Z schoolkids have repeatedly walked out of school on climate strikes, in a way that Millennial schoolkids never did, is a good example of how this generation are being shaped by the world they find themselves in. They are not looking for a compromise, or a 'best of both worlds' midpoint. They are looking for results.

Blake's awareness of the 'mind-forged manacles' that

usually bind our thinking helped him to see the injustices of the time clearly. They gave him an extended circle of empathy that left him unable to accept the prevailing societal values. In this, he was very similar to the networked 'woke' generation. Like them, he understood the importance of people coming together.

As Blake described the value of the New Church, founded by followers of the Swedish mystic Swedenborg, 'The Whole of the New Church is in the Active Life & not in Ceremonies at all.' What was important and spiritual about the Church, in other words, was not the rituals and ceremonies. It was that the rituals and ceremonies brought people together. As he wrote in *The Marriage of Heaven and Hell*, 'The bird a nest, the spider a web, man friendship.' We belong with others, in other words. This is entirely in keeping with his belief that closing ourselves off to other people is what creates our own Hell, and it is an idea that this group-minded, connected generation understand far better that the individualistic people of the twentieth century. The contemporary London poet Salena Godden, who spoke at the Extinction Rebellion protests, wrote that 'United as a people we are a million majestic colours, together we are a glorious stained-glass window. We are building a cathedral of otherness, brick by brick and book by book. This is the twenty-first century. We live in the future.' This is an entirely Blakean vision.

I think back to the aspects of Blake that the twentieth century latched on to, such as his belief in sexual liberation and his strong, anti-authoritarian individualism. These are still valid, but they have become part of a larger picture now. As our culture develops, we appreciate an increasing number of aspects of Blake's philosophy. It seems that as we grow and progress, we find that we understand him more.

I look down at Blake's words carved into stone around the top of Primrose Hill: 'I have conversed with the Spiritual Sun – I saw him on Primrose Hill.' Blake tells us that this spiritual sun is the blazing imagination, and that it is available right here, right now. It is not simple fantasy, but an imagination that is participatory, and which can alter the shape of the world. It can be used to make things better.

The words carved in stone at my feet remind me of his words carved into the grave marker in Bunhill Fields. We do not put up big statues or monuments to William Blake in this country. We don't really celebrate his birthplace. Instead we carve his words into rock and lower that rock into the ground, so that those words become London itself, or Albion, or Jerusalem. That is the ground on which we walk.

9

The Unfortunate Lunatic

The opening ceremony for the 2012 London Olympic Games was a wildly ambitious attempt to celebrate the entirety of British history and culture. Directed by the filmmaker Danny Boyle, it ranged over nearly four hours through pop music and children's literature to the industrial revolution, the digital revolution and the NHS. Nearly a billion people around the world tuned in to watch the ceremony that started off strange and, to international eyes, just kept getting weirder.

There had been a huge amount of cynicism in Britain before the Olympics thanks to the perceived incompetence of the organisers, the cost of development in a country undergoing a political programme of austerity, and the heavy corporate control of the games. Signs around the Olympic site with Orwellian corporate slogans such as 'We are proud to only accept VISA' created a feeling of foreboding. The fear was that the Olympic spirit had been lost.

The common assumption about the opening ceremony was that it would be awful. Viewers tuned in expecting to watch a national embarrassment. Instead, those wild, surreal hours proved to be an act of communal magic unlike anything else created in our lifetime. The country saw who they were in that ceremony, and with recognition came a sense of joy. Critics lined up to call it a masterpiece, but it was the effect on the country that really proved its value. The blanket of cynicism was pulled away from all but the most die-hard miserabilists. The Olympic spirit was suddenly everywhere, unmistakeable and unavoidable. The Olympics and Paralympics became a national party that lasted over a month and which nobody wanted to end.

Blake, of course, was a central part of all this. The opening segment to the ceremony was called 'Green and Pleasant Land'. The scene it depicted was inspired by his poem 'The Ecchoing Green', and 'Jerusalem' was sung in the stadium. The ceremony then went on to show the arrival of the 'dark Satanic mills', while the film *Chariots of Fire*, whose name was also inspired by the hymn 'Jerusalem', became the basis for a Mr Bean comedy sketch. The ceremony's writer Frank Cottrell Boyce had long looked to Blake for inspiration. He has since written a *Doctor Who* episode called 'In the Forest of the Night', a line from Blake's poem 'The Tyger'. As Danny Boyle described the aims of the ceremony in the brochure: 'Woven through it all, there runs a golden thread of purpose – the idea of Jerusalem – of a better world that can be built through the prosperity of industry, through the caring nation that built the welfare state, through the joyous energy of popular culture, through the dream of universal communication. We can build Jerusalem. And it will be for everyone.'

At the time of writing, seven years later, in the midst of the Brexit confusion, all this can seem like a long time ago. But it is worth putting the ceremony in a broader historical context. There is a long game playing out here.

In Blake's time, Britain was not a country known for imagination. This is, in part, why he was so unsuccessful during his life, and why his only critical review called him an 'unfortunate lunatic'. Britain was perceived as hard-working, a bit pig-headed, and uninspired. During Blake's lifetime the industrial revolution meant that we went from being seen as 'a nation of shopkeepers' to the 'workshop of the world'. While it's true that we had punched above our weight in literature ever since Chaucer, we were a long way behind the curve in other artistic pursuits, particularly painting and music. The vivid imagination that Blake championed had been largely absent, or even viewed with mistrust.

In the years since the Second World War, however, all this has changed. We now pride ourselves on being a creative country. We have given the world The Beatles, Harry Potter and *Grand Theft Auto*. We are globally recognised for our acting, fashion, music and art. Our writers are some of the best and most commercially successful in history, from Shakespeare, Jane Austen and Dickens, to Tolkien and Agatha Christie. Which other country can boast a globally famous anonymous graffiti artist? That we were able to express ourselves in an Olympics opening ceremony so imaginative and original is something that we now take for granted. But it is a recent phenomenon.

That this shift from a dull productive island to an island of creativity has largely gone unnoticed is due, in part, to how the hangover of Empire has distorted our sense of ourselves. We have been distracted from who we have become by the mirage of James Bond-style British exceptionalism, which assumes that we are somehow automatically better than other countries. Because we used to have a global empire, the thinking goes, we are still in some way more important than others. Wild delusions like this make it difficult to see who you really are, and also how much you have changed.

That competitive, antagonistic and obviously wrong view of the world is still being nurtured in exclusive private schools, whose pupils go on to have a disproportionate influence on the worlds of media, politics and academia. Being so far removed from the reality of life as it is experienced by the great majority, they maintain the belief that this island is, at its heart, sensible, noble, dutiful and classy, like the world depicted in *Downton Abbey*. But as a people, we are absolutely nothing like *Downton Abbey*. We are so different that it's a miracle that anyone could fall for this idea.

In these Brexit years, however, that long-lived illusion

has finally been destroyed for good. People the world over have been watching Britain in astonishment. As a Dutch journalist said to Jonathan Coe, 'We love Monty Python, but we always thought it was comedy, not a reality show.' The headline on the cover of the 17 June 2019 international edition of *Time* magazine was 'How Britain Went Bonkers'. The article inside began 'When did Britain go out of its mind?', as if all this were something new. 'Britain's nervous breakdown has its own unique loony flavour', it astutely noted.

Regardless of your political position, the Brexit saga has been a comedy of ineptitude, political amateurism and farce, and the greatest national embarrassment since the Suez Crisis. In the eyes of the world, Britain has gone from being the sort of stable, mature country that would never commit an act of national harm, to the crazy clownland that absolutely would do something like this. Spare a thought for how the rest of the world attempts to process our response to the rise of the far right, which is to throw milkshakes at people like Tommy Robinson and Nigel Farage. Britain, like Blake, is now seen as an 'unfortunate lunatic'.

There's no going back from here. Once the illusion has shattered, it cannot be repaired. The actions of the alumni of schools such as Eton, where the myth of British exceptionalism was long protected from reality, has destroyed the credibility of the ruling classes. They themselves may remain in denial about this for some time, but that doesn't really matter anymore. The

Downton Abbey myth of sensible, noble, dutiful and classy people has been so publicly destroyed that it can't be revived. In the networked twenty-first century, reputations can be shattered very quickly. They do not tend to recover.

This is not a bad thing. Free at last from the myth of British exceptionalism, we can at last see ourselves as we really are. This is what happened, for a few weeks anyway, after the 2012 London Olympics opening ceremony. The people on this island are a wild, psychedelic, eccentric, creative mob, as should have been blindingly obvious all along. We drink too much, have a very strange sense of humour, and are not short of original and potentially unwise ideas. We are the people who named a scientific research vessel Boaty McBoatface, and who still find that funny. We make films such as *The Wicker Man*, *Magical Mystery Tour* and *Monty Python and the Holy Grail*, and we invent musical movements such as punk, heavy metal, rave and grime. Eric Idle's 'Always Look on the Bright Side of Life' is one the ten most played songs at British funerals, and that sums us up nicely.

The *Downton Abbey* aspect of Britain, the world of butlers and silver forks, should not blind us to this. It does not contribute meaningfully to new and emerging modes of creative expression, such as the videogame industry or meme culture. This is not to say that it has never had value. Prior to the First World War, it played an important role in supporting and encouraging the creative growth of this country, and that history will always echo through to the present day. But now, it is just one of countless different flavours in our culture. It can no longer be claimed to be pre-eminent. It fails to explain or define us.

In the twenty-first century, this turns out to be hugely fortunate. Advances in AI and automation look set to take over practical, rational work, and a 'nation of shopkeepers' or the 'workshop of the world' will not do well in these times. Yet those machines are unable to replace us in areas that require imagination, creativity and irrational thinking. Our creative industries are growing at twice the rate of the rest of the economy and are now worth over a $100 billion a year. They are a major British export and provide 1 in 11 of all UK jobs. In May 2019, the then Foreign Secretary Jeremy Hunt suggested that a new royal yacht or plane would be a good way to promote Britain internationally in the post-Brexit future. This showed incredibly outdated thinking. What we really need is a new Beatles.

Blake was declaring the importance of deep imagination, and the world beyond our rational models, while his contemporaries were hailing the importance of reason. This put him out of sync with his own times and condemned him to a lifetime of obscurity, but it makes him entirely relevant to the modern world. Because our digital machines are the product of our rationality, they have defined limits. It is the unexplored landscape outside that closed rational territory where our skills are

JOHN HIGGS

needed. It is the imagination, as Coleridge defined it, where our work ahead lies.

The kind of blazing imagination that Blake possessed can be dangerous. It needs to be treated with respect, and wielding it effectively takes effort and practice. It can burn people out and can tip people into madness, especially if they are isolated – it needs to be balanced with things that are real and earthed. Now that we are the 'unfortunate lunatic', we will have to learn the skill of grounding ourselves in order to handle the mental energies involved. Blake's madness was Heavenly, but it is easy to allow paranoia, insecurity or bitterness to turn madness Hellish.

We should not hold up Blake himself as some form of saint, neither should we overlook his flaws. He showed signs of paranoia in later life, when his failure to find an audience was apparent, and he turned on friends who tried to help him. He was wrong about many things, especially worldly ones. He expressed the belief that the Earth was flat, for example, and denied that atoms could exist. His belief that there was more to the mind than the intellect blinded him to the importance of reason, which thankfully is a fault that Generation Z doesn't seem to share. But he never lost his belief in the primacy of the imagination, and he did not stop basking in that other sun until the end of his days. This is far more significant than any personal criticism we can make against him.

Because Blake's influence has slowly saturated our

culture, he has prepared us for the world we find ourselves in. We live in an imagined world now, and spend as much time in virtual space as we do in reality. We spend our evenings binging on story in the form of TV boxsets with 100-plus hours of narrative. Virtual reality and augmented reality are developing into powerful new ways to share our imagination with others. The art of the future is participatory, not passive. We have the tools to connect up our dreams, but it is our ideas that we need to focus on.

We need to understand the purpose of engaging with the light of that other, silent sun. It is not there to create simple amusement to pass the time. It is there to create a better world. It exists to collectively lift us all higher.

William Blake knew this. We have caught up to him to the extent that we are now seen as an 'unfortunate lunatic'. Clearly, we are getting somewhere.

Notes and Sources

The references to Blake's words are all taken from *The Complete Poetry & Prose of William Blake: Newly Revised Edition*, edited by David V. Erdman (Doubleday, 1988), which is referred to below as 'CPP'.

1. The Unveiling

The Bunhill Fields Burial Ground is at 38 City Road, London EC1Y 2BG. Blake's new grave marker, which is harder to find than the earlier stone marking his 'nearby' resting place, is in the south-eastern corner of the northern lawn. Details of The Blake Society can be found at www.blakesociety.org. The lyrics to the hymn 'Jerusalem' are taken from the preface to Blake's *Milton: A Poem in 2 Books* (CPP p95), and not, as might be assumed, from his book *Jerusalem: The Emanation of The Giant Albion*.

The quote from Chris Bateman is taken from p.57 of his book *Imaginary Games* (Zero Books, 2011). The illustration of a star landing on Blake's foot is on plate 29 of *Milton: A Poem in 2 Books*. Blake was described as 'an unfortunate lunatic' by Robert Hunt in the 17

September 1809 edition of the radical newspaper *The Examiner.*

The quote from Blake beginning 'I give you the end of a golden string' is from plate 77 of *Jerusalem: The Emanation of the Giant Albion* (CPP, p.231). The description of Blake's childhood vision of a tree full of angels at Peckham Rye, with their 'bright angelic wings bespangling every bough like stars', comes from p.7 of Alexander Gilchrist's *Life of William Blake* (Macmillan and Co., 1863).

2. The Twentieth Century

The quote telling us that Blake's 'name and his work are but indifferently known' is from p.1 of Irene Langridge's *William Blake: A Study of his Life and Art Work* (George Bell and Sons, 1904). The quotes from Allen Ginsberg regarding his Blake vision are from his 1965 interview with Thomas Clark, published in *The Paris Review*, issue 37, spring 1966.

Blake's poem 'Ah! Sun-Flower' is from *Songs of Experience* (CPP, p.25). For a fuller account of the influence of Ginsberg and Aldous Huxley on Timothy Leary, see my book *I Have America Surrounded: The Life of Timothy Leary* (The Friday Project, 2006).

Blake's quote about 'the doors of perception' is from plate 14 of *The Marriage of Heaven and Hell* (CPP, p.39). Patti Smith recounts Robert Mapplethorpe's destruction of a Blake print on p.50 of *Just Kids* (Bloomsbury, 2010).

'Those who restrain desire, do so because theirs is weak enough to be restrained' is from *The Marriage of Heaven and Hell* (CPP, p.34), as is 'The road of excess leads to the palace of wisdom' (CPP, p.35). For a full account of Blake's influence on 1960s counterculture, see *William Blake and the Age of Aquarius* by Stephen F. Eisenman *et al* (Princeton University Press, 2017).

3. London

Blake's poem 'London' is from *Songs of Experience* (CPP, p.26). The quotes from *Milton: A Poem in 2 Books*, which begin 'Rouze up, O Young Men of the New Age!' and 'I will not cease from Mental Fight', are both from plate 1 (CPP, p.95). 'A War Song to Englishmen' is from Blake's early collection *Poetical Sketches* (CPP, p.440), while 'When Klopstock England Defied' was written in Blake's notebook but never published in his lifetime (CPP, p.500).

The lines beginning 'And all must love the human form' are from 'The Divine Image' in *Songs of Innocence* (CPP, p.13). 'Without Contraries is no progression' is from plate 3 of *The Marriage of Heaven and Hell* (CPP, p.34), while 'Opposition is true friendship', although barely legible in some painted copies, is from the bottom of plate 20 (CPP, p.42).

4. Blake Now

Professor Jason Whitaker can be found on Twitter as

@Blake2_0. His blog, zoamorphosis.com, is also highly recommended. Blake's Proverbs of Hell can be found in plates 7 to 10 of *The Marriage of Heaven and Hell* (CPP, pp.35–8). 'Fiery the angels rose' is from *America: A Prophecy* (CPP, p.55).

The quote from an online review of *Devil May Cry* 5 comes from Callum Agnew's 7 February 2019 article on wccftech.com, '*Devil May Cry* 5 Hands-on Preview – V Is Just Too Much Fun'. The quote beginning 'In a horrible, dreamful slumber' is from *The First Book of Urizen* (CPP, p.75).

5. *Understanding Blake*

The reference to Catherine Blake's inability to understand her husband's work comes from an 1830 essay by Allan Cunningham, reprinted on p.638 of G.E. Bentley Jr's *Blake Records: Second Edition* (Yale University Press, 2004). The quote from Peter Ackroyd is from p.4 of his book *Blake* (Sinclair Stevenson, 1995). The quote from Jah Wobble is taken from the 4 June 2009 *New Statesman* article 'Perspectives: Jah Wobble, musician, on William Blake'.

Julian Cope's speech marked the opening of the exhibition *Blake's Shadow: William Blake and his Artistic Legacy*, which was at The Whitworth Art Gallery from 26 January to 20 April 2008. The quotes from Bruce Dickinson are from p.269 of his autobiography *What Does This Button Do?* (Harper Collins, 2017), and his version of 'Jerusalem' can be found on his 1998 solo album *Chemical Wedding*, along other Blake-influenced songs such as 'Gates of Urizen' and 'Book of Thel'.

6. On Being Remembered

The exhibition *Tracey Emin and William Blake in Focus* was at Tate Liverpool from 16 September 2016 to 3 September 2017. The quote from Neal Brown is taken from p.10 of his book *Tracey Emin* (Tate Publishing, 2006). Blake's quote beginning 'I come to Self Annihilation' is from *Milton: Book the Second* (CPP, p.139).

7. Once Only Imagin'd

'What is now proved was once only imagin'd' is from *The Marriage of Heaven and Hell* (CPP, p.36). The quote from Einstein is taken from p.97 of his 1931 book *Cosmic Religion: With Other Opinions and Aphorisms*. Samuel Taylor Coleridge coined the word 'esemplastic' in his 1817 work *Biographia Literaria*.

'In your Bosom you bear your Heaven and Earth & all you behold' is from *Jerusalem: Chapter 3* (CPP p225), while the extract from 'The Everlasting Gospel' is from CPP, p.524. 'Men forgot that all deities reside in the human breast' is from *The Marriage of Heaven and Hell* (CPP, p.38). The quote from Henry Crabb Robinson's diary is from 10 December 1825 and can be found on p.421 of *Blake Records: Second Edition*, by G. E. Bentley Jr (Yale University Press, 2004).

8. On Primrose Hill

The 'Iolo – Who He?' editorial in a 2009 edition of the *Friends of Regent's Park and Primrose Hill* quarterly magazine was written by Malcolm Kafetz. The story of Allen Ginsberg's visit to Primrose Hill is recounted in Iain Sinclair's small book *Blake's London: The Topographic Sublime* (The Swedenborg Society, 2018). Blake's letter to Thomas Butts is dated 22 November 1802 (CPP, pp.720–22).

'Then the Divine Vision like a silent Sun appear'd above' is from *Jerusalem: Chapter 2* (CPP, p.191). The poem 'London' is from *Songs of Experience* (CPP, p.26). 'Without Contraries is no progression' is from *The Marriage of Heaven and Hell* (CPP, p.34). For a more detailed discussion of metamodernism, see chapter 4 of my book *The Future Starts Here: Adventures in the Twenty-First Century* (Weidenfeld and Nicolson, 2019).

Blake wrote 'The Whole of the New Church is in the Active Life & not in Ceremonies at all' as an annotation in Swedenborg's *Divine Love and Divine Wisdom* (CPP, p.605). 'The bird a nest, the spider a web, man friendship' is from *The Marriage of Heaven and Hell* (CPP, p.36). The quote from Salena Godden is from her essay 'Shade' in *The Good Immigrant*, edited by Nikesh Shukla (Unbound, 2016). Crabb Robinson recorded Blake saying, 'I have conversed with the Spiritual Sun – I saw him on Primrose Hill', in his diary on 10 December 1825.

9. The Unfortunate Lunatic

The quote from Danny Boyle is from his short essay 'Isles of Wonder' on p.11 of the *London 2012 Olympic Games Opening Ceremony Media Guide*. Blake was described as an 'unfortunate lunatic' by Robert Hunt in the 17 September 1809 issue of *The Examiner*. Jonathan Coe reported the comments of an unnamed Dutch journalist on his Twitter account on 7 March 2019. The quotes from the 17 June 2019 international edition of *Time* Magazine are by Tina Brown and taken from her article 'How Britain Lost the Plot Over Brexit'.

Further Reading

The complete works of Blake are easily available. For anyone wishing to begin exploring these, the places to start are *William Blake: The Complete Illuminated Works* (Thames and Hudson, 2000) and *William Blake: The Complete Poems* (Penguin, 1977). The best and most accessible biography is still Peter Ackroyd's *Blake* (Sinclair Stevenson, 1995), while all of Blake's artwork can be found at the Blake Archive website (blakearchive.org). I would recommend starting with *The Marriage of Heaven and Hell*.

For those exploring further, the key reference books are *The Complete Poetry & Prose of William Blake: Newly Revised Edition*, edited by David V. Erdman (Doubleday, 1988), *Blake Records: Second Edition*, by G. E. Bentley, Jr (Yale University Press, 2004) and *A Blake Dictionary: The Ideas and Symbols of William Blake* by S. Foster Damon (Dartmouth College Press, 2013). The Blake Society (www.blakesociety.org) is also well worth joining.

There are countless books of academic literary criticism analysing Blake's work through every lens imaginable. It is no doubt a foolish task to try to single one out as particularly helpful, but I am certainly a great fan of *Witness Against the Beast: William Blake and the Moral Law*, by E. P. Thompson (The New Press, 1993).

Blake keeps appearing in modern culture in unpredictable and varied ways. He is a constant presence in *Drive Your Plow Over the Bones of the Dead*, a dark, feminist murder mystery novel written by the Polish author Olga Tokarczuk in 2009, which was translated into English in 2018. In Jim Jarmusch's black-and-white film noir western *Dead Man* (1995), Johnny Depp stars as a lost soul believed to be William Blake by his Native American guide. Blake can also be found in Brian Catling's *The Vorrh* trilogy, especially in its third volume, which is an extraordinary fantasy about an ancient sentient forest that contains the Garden of Eden.

Acknowledgements

Huge thanks to Paul Murphy, Jenny Lord, Jo Whitford, Virginia Woolstencroft, Sarah Ballard and Eli Keren for making it happen, and to Joanne Mallon, Jason Arnopp, Alistair Fruish and David Bramwell for braving the very first draft and providing notes and wisdom.

Special thanks to Professor Jason Whittaker, his @blake2_0 Twitter account and his zoamorphosis.com website, which have all been invaluable guides to the presence of William Blake in the twenty-first century.